Little Pebble™

Simple Machines

Inclined Planes

by Martha E. H. Rustad

raintree

a Capstone company — publishers for children

Raintree is an imprint of Capstone Global Library Limited, a company incorporated in England and Wales having its registered office at 264 Banbury Road, Oxford, OX2 7DY – Registered company number: 6695582

www.raintree.co.uk
myorders@raintree.co.uk

Edited by Marissa Kirkman
Designed by Kyle Grentz (cover) and Charmaine Whitman (interior)
Original illustrations © Capstone Global Library Limited 2018
Picture research by Jo Miller
Production by Katy LaVigne
Originated by Capstone Global Library Limited
Printed and bound in India.

ISBN 978 1 4747 5361 6
21 20 19 18 17
10 9 8 7 6 5 4 3 2 1

British Library Cataloguing in Publication Data
A full catalogue record for this book is available from the British Library.

Acknowledgements
We would like to thank the following for permission to reproduce photographs: Capstone Studio: Karon Dubke, 17, 21; iStockphoto: /kali9, 11, Shinyfamily, 15; Science Source: Photo Researchers, Inc., 7; Shutterstock: BCFC, 9, Caron Badkin, 13, Grandpa, 22, Marcel Derweduwen, cover, 1, Sajee Rod, 5, wavebreakmedia, 19

Contents

Help with work

Work is hard!

We need help.

Use a simple machine.

These tools help us work.

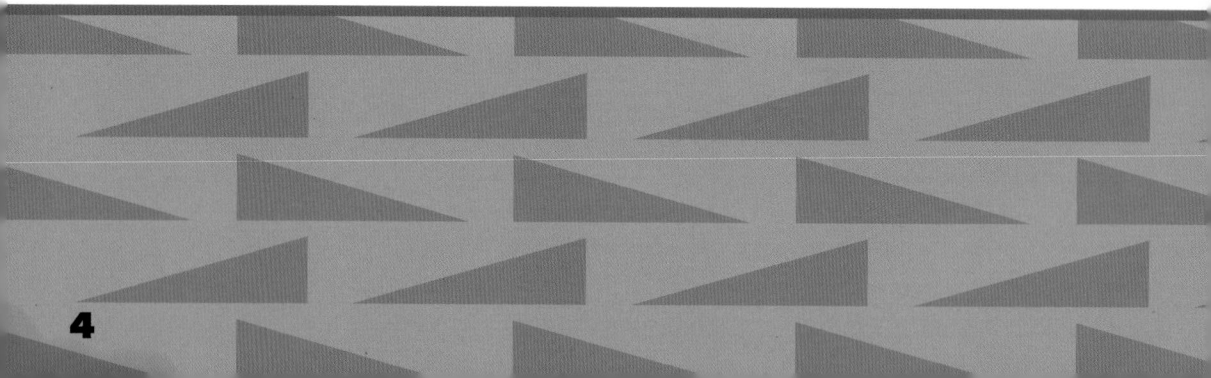

inclined plane
4

An inclined plane is a ramp. We move a load up or down the ramp.

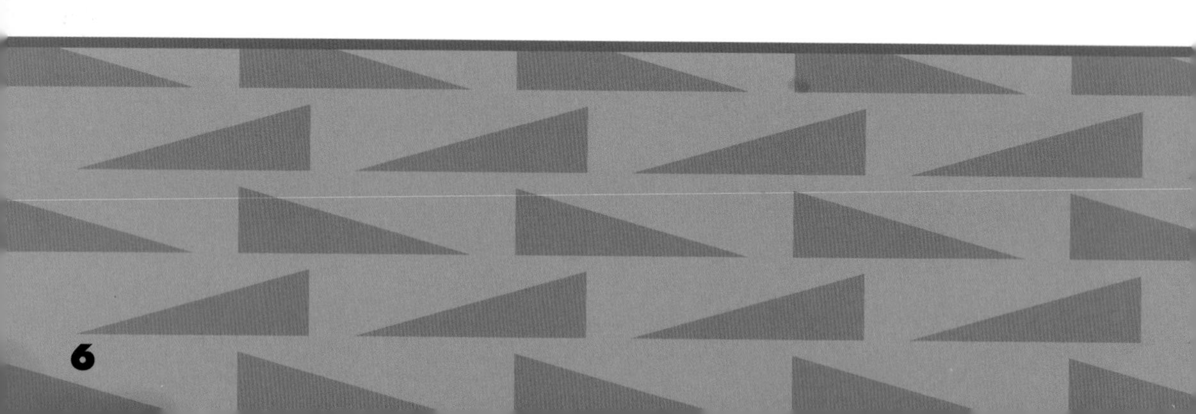

load
ramp

Move a load

One end is low.

The other end is high.

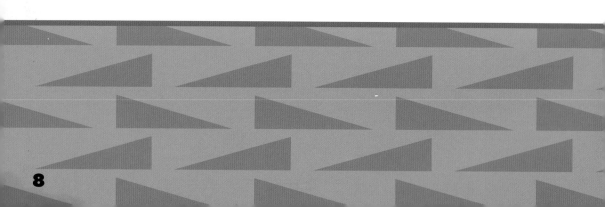

A load sits at the bottom.

We move it up.

load

The load moves to the top.

It takes longer to get there.

But the work is easier.

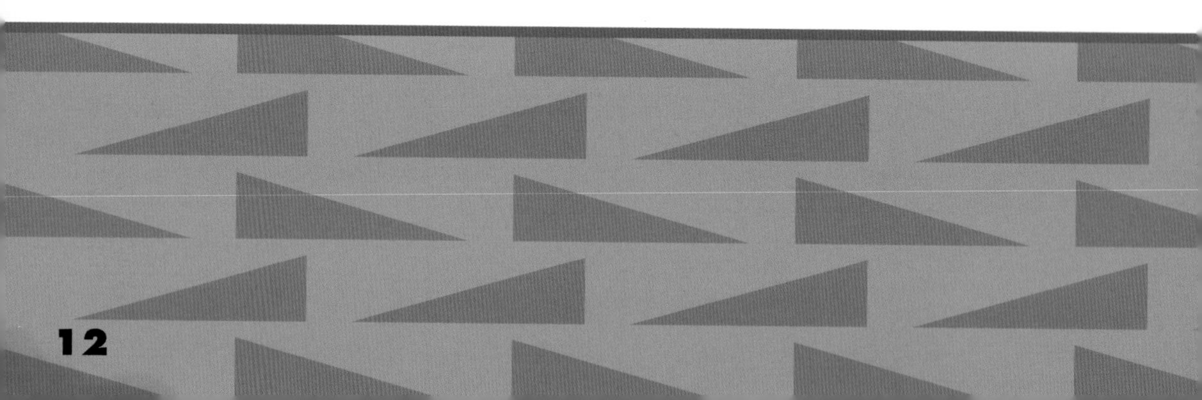

211-1168

Everyday tools

The train is at the bottom.

Push!

The train goes up the ramp.

A slide is an inclined plane.

Whee!

I zoom down.

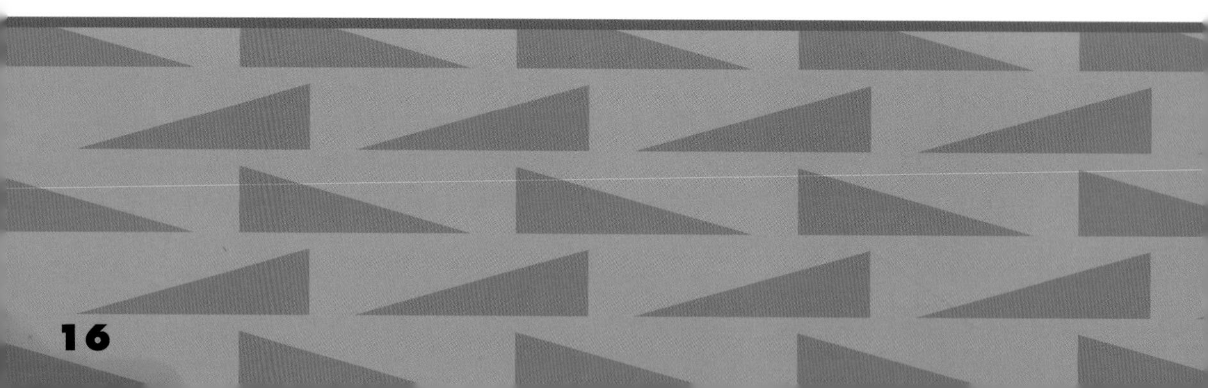

Steps are an inclined plane.

Climb!

We can reach the top.

We use a simple machine.

It makes work easier and fun.

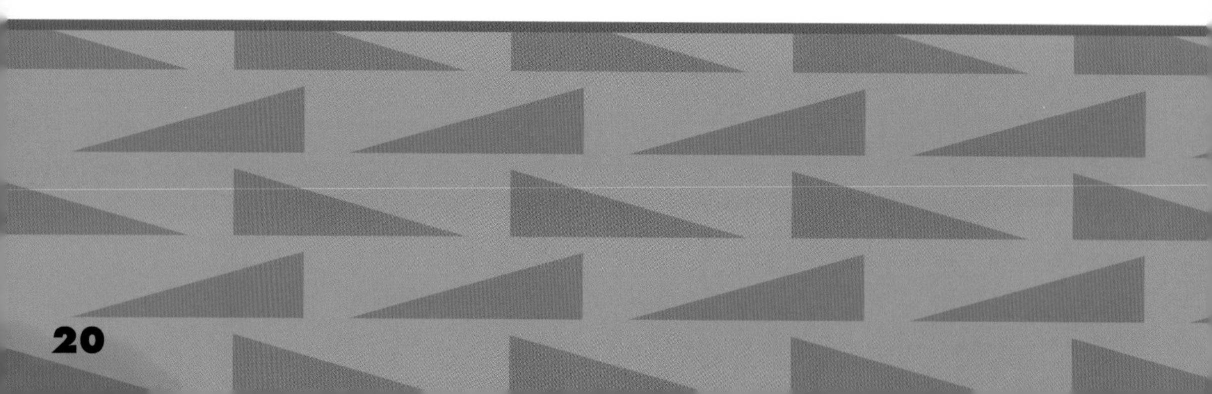

Glossary

inclined plane simple machine that makes moving a load up or down easier; it is sloped with one end higher than the other, like a ramp

load object that you want to move or lift

simple machine tool that makes it easier to do something

tool item used to make work easier

work job that must be done

Read more

Fred Flintstone's Adventures with Inclined Planes: A Rampin' Good Time (Flintstones Explain Simple Machines), Mark Weakland (Capstone Press, 2016)

Making Machines with Ramps and Wedges (Simple Machine Projects), Chris Oxlade (Raintree, 2016)

The Kids' Book of Simple Machines: Cool Projects and Activities That Make Science Fun, Kelly Doudna (Mighty Media Kids, 2015)

Websites

www.bbc.co.uk/guides/zptckqt#zgb7xnb
Explore simple machines with Seymour on the BBC website.

www.rigb.org/index.php?url=%2Ffamilies%2Fexperimental%2Ffor-5-8-year-olds
Investigate science at home with simple experiments on The Royal Institution's website for children.

Comprehension questions

1. What do we move up or down a ramp?
2. What is different about the two ends of an inclined plane?
3. What types of inclined planes have you used? How did they help you?

Index